Strands of Hope: How to Grieve the Loss of a Horse

Susan Friedland

Strands of Hope: How to Grieve the Loss of a Horse

© 2020 Susan Friedland

Saddle Seeks Horse Press
All rights reserved.

Cover Design: Amy Summer Ellison
Editor: Holly Caccamise
Photos: Carolyn Rikje and Dana White; back cover photo by Kerri Weiss

ISBN: 978-1-7327105-2-8
Print Edition

Susan Friedland
saddleseekshorse.com

Susan Friedland

STRANDS OF HOPE: HOW TO GRIEVE THE LOSS OF A HORSE

Susan Friedland, an award-winning equestrian blogger at Saddle Seeks Horse, is a middle school teacher by day and horse girl 24/7. Susan's first book *Horses Adored and Men Endured: a Memoir of Falling and Getting Back Up* debuted in 2018, gaining an enthusiastic following and has garnered praise from *UnTacked*, *Horse and Style*, *The Midwest Equestrian* and Jean Abernethy, the creator of Fergus the Horse. Saddle Seeks Horse, Susan's blog born out of horse shopping, features a mix of product reviews, riding inspiration and adventures with her OTTB Tiz A Knight, a newbie field hunter. Susan's writing about horses and the people who love them has appeared in *Horse Illustrated* and *Sidelines* and on various equestrian websites. Connect with Susan via her blog, or email if you ever want to talk horse.

saddleseekshorse.com
susan@saddleseekshorse.com

Blessed are those who mourn, for they will be comforted.
Matthew 5:4
The Bible, New International Version

This book is written in memory of my heart horse DC who brought joy to so many people.

This book is dedicated to my family for their ongoing love and support, and my fellow horse lovers who have known the pain of losing a beloved horse.

Contents

Introduction

I'M SO SORRY.

My guess is that you or someone close to you has recently lost a horse, which is how you found this book.

The pain of losing one's best equine friend is a very real thing. And it's not just a metaphorical pain. I remember that socked-in-the-gut feeling accompanied with emptiness and bewilderment when I lost my heart horse DC to colic in 2010. He was 23.

He'd just had a thorough vet check a few months earlier to see if he was healthy enough to travel by trailer from Illinois to California in order to relocate with me. The vet said, "He doesn't know how old he is. He's in great shape. Keep working him."

I had owned my beautiful bay Thoroughbred gelding for 16 years, and he journeyed with me through post-college young adulthood. We moved to California from the Midwest, I went to grad school, had a career change, and endured years of singleness with hopes of meeting a good man, but I kept hitting dead ends. He was my steady companion, best listener, and a constant source of joy both in and out of the saddle.

He was more than a pet. He was my heart horse.

The day DC died, I didn't want to eat. I literally had no appetite for most of the day. I love food, so that was really unusual for me. I didn't know if I should go to work or call in sick and stay home. I was bereaved.

I felt like the rug had been pulled out from under me, and I wasn't sure what to do with myself.

It took time, but I figured it out.

There is no one right path to grieve the loss of a horse, and each horse person deals with loss differently. I'm not a psychologist or minister (I'm actually a teacher by profession).

I don't have any wild aspirations that I can help you "get over it." I am simply sharing my experiences and ideas that helped me process the painful loss and try to heal so I could smile again and eventually ride and be around horses without having the barn be a trigger—a painful reminder of my horse that was no more.

I have found several kindred spirit horse lovers who have also grieved a horse and have been willing to share their experiences in the hopes that you will feel less alone. Their individual circumstances range from losing a foal to losing a beloved childhood pony and beyond. There's even a chapter dedicated to one horsewoman's experience having to retire her very young show jumper. Granted, he is still alive and well, but she had to grieve the death of her dream to compete at the highest levels with her just-getting-started partner.

In 2018, I received an email from a mom in South Africa who was writing to thank me for publishing the blog post "How to Grieve a Horse in 10 Not-So-Easy Steps" on my blog Saddle Seeks Horse. Her adolescent daughter had unexpectedly lost her pony and mom had somehow landed on my writing and it resonated with her.

She said that in reading my blog post, she and her daughter felt less alone. My words gave them a bit of comfort.

Did you catch that? She said *they felt less alone.*

I can't take away your pain, but I can share my experiences and a few from fellow horse lovers to remind you that you are not alone, and impress on you that in time, you'll be okay. **You are not alone.**

Every person is unique, so this is not a "do these things and you'll feel better" formula. There is no fast track to banishing the pain of losing a horse. Think of the information contained in these pages as sisterly advice. Take what is helpful and leave the rest. Feel free to skim and scan this book. Some parts will resonate with you more than others.

At the end of each chapter in Part I, I have included optional assignments. Sometimes when I feel bad, if I can just do something—be active—I feel a little better. So that's the purpose behind each assignment. Complete them all if you wish, or simply choose the ones that feel right for you.

You are not alone, and what you are going through is beyond difficult, but in time it will get better. Meanwhile persevere in the best way you can—whatever that looks like for you now. I hope this book provides a small measure of comfort in the midst of your sorrow.

Remember, you are not alone.

My good boy DC. Owned & loved from 1994-2010.

PART ONE

CHAPTER 1

Cry

"WHAT WOULD YOU do if he were your horse?" I asked, not really wanting the answer from the vet I had never met, but who had been overseeing my distressed horse for the previous few hours from 2,000 miles away in Illinois.

I wasn't present to assess the situation, but put my trust in a woman who I assumed also possessed my same heart for horses. She reluctantly said if DC, my tall bay dream on four hooves, were her horse, she would euthanize him. And she said she was very sorry.

I never had the chance to say goodbye to my longtime companion. I was in California. Horses sometimes colic, have freak accidents or get sick. It's one of the risks of loving them.

I cried for days and weeks after my sweet DC died. I remember it feeling like a literal weight was on my body. Truth be told, there are times when I still cry. It's just much less frequent now.

I'm not generally much of a crier, possessing a rather stoic, Midwestern farming heritage. But I made up for it following DC's death on November 1, 2010.

I cried because I missed DC. I cried because he was a piece of my history that I felt connected to. I was in my early 20s when I bought him, and when he exited my life, I was at the threshold of middle age. In grieving my gorgeous horse, I grieved the loss of my youth. I felt like those 16 years vanished when he breathed his last breath.

I've cried many times as I have written posts on my blog Saddle Seeks Horse. Just thinking about DC or looking at an old picture triggers my emotions and tears. In fact, I delayed publishing *Horses Adored and Men Endured: a Memoir of Falling and Getting Back Up* for years because I knew that in order to bring my tales of bad dates and awesome horses to life, I'd have to write about DC's death. I'd have to "go there" in my memory to that fateful early morning phone call from the barn manager telling me something wasn't right.

I'm not sure when, but at some point I decided to stop feeling silly for crying over "just a horse," because he was more than an animal I'd owned for 16 years. He was a confidante, comedian, and partner in many adventures, to name just a few roles he held.

Maybe you're someone who is less averse to showing emotion through tears. You've got the crying part down and it's already helping you. I had heard over the years that "crying is good for you" and "crying is healthy." I knew that in a general sense but was pretty amazed to find out some specifics on how crying helps us.

Health Benefits of Tears

According to an article from *Psychology Today*, "Crying is. . . essential to resolve grief, when waves of tears periodically come over us after we experience a loss. Tears help us process the loss so we can keep living with open hearts. Otherwise, we are set up for depression if we suppress these potent feelings."[1]

As much as I don't love crying, I do want to be a person who lives with an open heart—someone who can process a loss, rather than gloss over it. Maybe you're that way too.

Did you know there are three types of tears we humans cry? Of the three, grief tears actually excrete stress hormones. They literally have a different chemical composition than tears we shed say, cutting an onion or from elation!

I also found out some people in Japan are so enthusiastic about the health benefits of crying that certain cities have opened "crying clubs" called *rui-katsu*. The literal translation of the word *rui-katsu* means "tear-seeking."[2] I have never been to one, but apparently people congregate in these clubs to connect with each other and have a good old-fashioned cry. To initiate the crying, sad movies are played.

Japanese culture has embraced tears for overall health. Perhaps we equestrians should too.

The Beauty of Tears

Someone very close to me tends to apologize when she cries. I don't think apologies for crying are ever necessary (well, maybe if you are crying crocodile tears—you know, the fake ones used to manipulate people). Tears are a means of expression and communicating our hearts, whether happy or sad. I was recently blown away when I learned another fascinating fact about human tears.

Tears are actually stunning works of art. Yes, tears themselves are beautiful and unique. Photographer Rose-Lynn Fischer entered a season of grief after losing a friend, and tears were common. She wondered if different types of tears looked different from each other. Fischer began capturing some of her own tears and those of others, placing them on slides to examine under a microscope. She embarked on a project to photograph different tear varieties. The result is her book *The Topography of Tears*.[3]

Some of the tears look like snowflakes and have intricate, symmetrical patterns. Others resemble winter landscapes with a row of barren, gnarled trees. Still others look like views from an airplane window when traveling over various fields of crops. You can see some of her mysterious photographs on her website,
www.rose-lynnfisher.com/tears.html.

I am a Christian and believe we have a loving Creator, so learning about the exquisiteness and individuality of tears was surprising, but not shocking. It made me think back to the time when I was at a museum and saw a tiny, oblong container about the size of a Sharpie cap. It was a tear bottle, also known as a lachrymatory. In ancient cultures, these bottles were found buried alongside the deceased. Presumably the bereaved filled the tiny bottle with tears as a way to symbolize the loss and grief.

There is a reference in one of the Psalms in the Bible to God storing up David's tears. It's poetic language to show deep devotion and attentiveness to our sorrow. Regardless of your faith background or lack thereof, the mere existence of lachrymatory as artifacts tells the story that tears have historically been valued and precious. The tears you shed over a horse are valuable and precious, so allow them to flow freely.

Chapter 1 "Cry" Optional Assignment

- Peruse Rose-Lynn Fischer's website and observe the varying designs of tears.
- If you want a greater challenge, tell a loved one about the tears' topography or try sketching what you think your tears might look like if placed under a microscope.

CHAPTER 2

Do the Things

THE MORNING WE had to euthanize DC I said to my husband, "I don't know what I'm supposed to do right now." Remember, DC was in Illinois and I was in California. He said I should go to work—that staying home wouldn't help anything. I knew he was right, but the shock of what was happening was too much to take in. I felt stymied, and I seriously needed him to guide me in my actions since I couldn't think.

I know that it's common in the workplace to allow employees who've lost a family member to take personal days in order to attend to the details of a funeral and such. My horse was family, but I knew it wouldn't technically qualify as an excused grief leave. But I wasn't sure I would be able to be effective in my job.

I made it to school, crying for most of my hour commute (back to the crying). When I arrived, I remember feeling a sense of relief. While in my classroom, interacting with students, it was like play acting. I didn't tell my students of my tragedy and I went through my day just like any other. While I was engaged with my class, my brain couldn't "go there," meaning I was able to have a breather from my grief. Keeping to my normal routine was helpful.

My husband suggested we go out to dinner that night. It was a nice break from cooking, and having someone else serve us was helpful as it required zero energy on my part. I remember as plain as day his prayer before we ate, thanking God for the wonderful years I had with DC. And the savory dill rice and chicken enchilada tasted amazing after not wanting to eat all day.

If you're up to being in public, it's not a bad idea to treat yourself to a good meal at your favorite restaurant. The change that results in the loss of a horse is a stressful life event, so why not pamper yourself a little bit with a meal that you don't have to plan for, prepare and then clean up afterward?

Now some people find cooking to be a relaxing and de-stressing activity. I'm not one of those people, but if you are, maybe whipping up a special meal will be helpful to you. By immersing yourself in a menu and dinner, perhaps it will ease the sting, if only temporarily.

Besides work and eating, try to keep up with your other life commitments. For example, if you regularly go to the gym, don't give up on it. If you need to walk the dog, walk the dog. If you're in a book club, go to book club. Activity is good for you in the season of loss. As much as you are able, try to maintain normalcy in your schedule and routine.

Chapter 2 "Do the Things" Optional Assignment

- Look at your calendar and highlight two commitments in the next two weeks that you know you should keep because it will be good for you.

- If you want a greater challenge, schedule a "pick me up" now. This might be a day at the spa getting pampered, or maybe going on that hiking trail you've always wanted to explore. Perhaps there's a new restaurant in town you keep hearing good things about. Maybe you haven't seen a play in years. Indulge yourself.

CHAPTER 3

Share and Remember

THE DAY DC died, after calling my parents and sisters to tell them about my loss, the first person I shared my devastating news with in person was a teacher who was a fellow horse owner. I knew he would understand exactly what I was going through because he's owned several horses throughout the course of his life. One of his special horses was actually sired by the horse used in the Lone Ranger series! He didn't say much, but his hug and "I'm sorry" communicated empathy. I wasn't sure how to bring it up to my non-horsey coworkers, but I was pleasantly surprised.

Tell the Non-Horse People

If you haven't already, I'm going to encourage you to take a risk and tell the non-horse people in your life about the loss of your horse. You just might be surprised at how empathetic they can be. Just because they're not one of the truly horse-obsessed doesn't mean they can't commiserate.

Depending on your situation in life, whether you're a student or stay-at-home mom, educator like me or have a job in a workplace outside of your home, you might encounter the non-horsey folks in your life in person before you see your horse friends. I would encourage you to not be shy about your loss. Here's what happened in my situation.

About halfway through that horrible day DC died, I confided in another teacher about his unexpected death. She knew I had a horse, and I knew she wasn't a horse person. I was not close friends with her, yet her compassionate response astonished me!

This fellow English teacher seemed to grasp the full weight of my sorrow. In fact, she even offered to teach my afternoon classes for me. I remember her saying, "Just go home. I can cover for you." She gave me the gift of being able to leave early without having to take official time off of work. Her generosity was comforting.

Before I told her my devastating secret, I think I was afraid that she would be dismissive since she wasn't a horse person.

I underestimated her. Her kind response made me feel safe in further retelling my sad tale. It opened the door for me to be authentic with more of my coworkers.

Would you believe there was not a single non-horse person I shared my loss with over the next few days who tried to diminish my sadness? In every retelling of my tragedy with non-equestrians, I received sincere apologies and frequently hugs.

The depth of a relationship with a horse might not be

something that the non-horse person will identify with, but we have all had some loss in life. Be open to the comfort of others who know you even if you don't think they will "get it." You just might be surprised.

When Lady Gaga's horse passed away in early 2019, the pop icon posted a picture of her riding the gray Arabian mare on her Instagram. It got over 1.6 million likes and 22,000 comments. Presumably not all of her fans are horse people, but they empathized, expressing condolences for their star's loss. By reaching out to Lady Gaga, they were able to show devotion to an entertainer they care about.

In much the same way, telling our story of loss whether in person, through email, or on social media allows the opportunity for our friends, fans, and acquaintances to express their solidarity.

Write a Eulogy

When DC died, I felt I owed it to many people to share the story of my loss. Over the course of sixteen years, he met and left a mark on many people, from barn owners in Illinois and California to shareboarders and close friends of mine who had also known, loved and ridden him.

A few days later I sat down to write and composed a full-blown horse eulogy. I emailed it to my close family, friends, and anyone I'd known from previous barns over the years who'd had a connection with DC and me.

In response, I received the most beautiful, encouraging words. It felt good knowing I was not the only one who loved that horse. Having little pieces of other people's sadness to mix in with my own huge vat was some comfort. I knew I wasn't alone.

The owner of a small, private barn I had boarded DC at in Southern California emailed me back almost immediately and told me DC was special, and often at night as she went around to check on the horses before bedtime, she would give him a carrot or some other treat. I had been out of touch with this woman for over ten years. My heart and eyes swelled with this new revelation of someone else's affection for my beloved horse.

I received another email back from my friend Suzanne. I met Suzanne at the barn when she too owned a young OTTB and DC and I were a new partnership. Suzanne and I rode together on many cold winter evenings in Illinois and at summer horse shows at Lamplight Equestrian Center. One summer when I was traveling for a couple of weeks, she rode DC for me. She took him out on trails, and her rides were actually like training rides. Suzanne really knew my horse and loved him as though he were her own.

Susan,

Thank you for sharing your news about DC. I've got tears in my eyes; this could be my story with my horse. You expressed so many of the same feelings that I have about him. He too, has been a constant friend in my life. You could add up all of the costs and expenses of keeping them over the years, but their friendship is PRICELESS.

Although there are a growing number of gray hairs on his forehead, he's in great shape and peo-

ple are amazed when I tell them his age. I believe regular riding, lots of pasture turnout and TLC keeps him young.

Again, thank you for sharing... you'll see him in heaven one day. I honestly believe God's timing is amazing... it was time for your dear friend DC to go. I guess I like to think of it that way.

Blessings and love.

What if I share my loss and get pat answers or dismissive responses?

Don't dwell on dumb things people say. Not everyone you know oozes empathy. Some people are socially clueless; they can't help themselves. Most people do have good hearts and so just give them the benefit of the doubt they were trying to be comforting and helpful.

Jeannine Moga shares in her paper written for the University of Minnesota Equine Center *Coping with the Loss of a Horse,* "Humans fear and avoid death because it is simply too big to wrap our brains around. Many people may offer well-meaning, but ill-timed and off-putting, advice to those who have lost a horse. If this happens to you, thank them kindly for their thoughts and then find support from others who resist the temptation to offer a 'quick fix'. Horses are not appliances to be replaced but loved ones to be mourned and honored."[4]

When sharing the loss of your horse, if you come across folks who don't understand that "horses are loved ones to be mourned and honored," as Moga puts it, keep your head up high and move on. I get you, and countless horse lovers around the world get you too. Remember, you are not alone.

Chapter 3 "Share and Remember" Optional Assignment

- Share the story of your horse and how much he or she meant to you with a few non-horse people.
- If you want a greater challenge, read the eulogy I wrote for my horse DC in Appendix A and then go to the Horse Eulogy Template in Appendix B, and write a eulogy for your horse. Consider sharing your eulogy with all the friends you and your horse knew from over the years. (By the way, I'd be honored to read your eulogy too. My email is susan@saddleseekshorse.com.)

CHAPTER 4

Embrace Your Grief

DON'T FEEL GUILTY being sad over a horse. I'll say it again.

Don't feel guilty being sad over a horse.

In the wake of losing DC, I struggled with feeling guilty that I was so distressed over losing a horse.

Who was I to feel like my whole world had fallen apart when other people had it so much worse in life, whether by losing a spouse or child, job or health?

I thought on a grand scale about people in the world who were experiencing deep pain and ongoing tragedy—people like refugees, child laborers working in factories, those who are trafficked for sex, people persecuted for their religious faith, etc., and felt like my problem of losing a horse was so small compared to real PROBLEMS. I felt like being devastated by the death of my special horse was definitely a #firstworldproblem.

I can't remember which friend assured me it was okay to feel my feelings on this one, but someone set me straight insisting that it's okay to mourn loss—it's part of the human experience. There is nothing to be ashamed of in feeling the loss of a beloved horse on a deep level.

Avoid Comparison

Don't compare your grief to others' grief. You are unique, your relationship with your horse was special, and there isn't another horse-human partnership in the world quite like the one you had.

Everyone grieves at his or her own pace. During my time with Knight, my heart horse number two, the only times I've cried about DC were when I was at my desk finishing the manuscript of my memoir *Horses Adored and Men Endured.* I had to in a sense "go there" in my mind and recreate the scene of that day of the unwelcome phone call and then replay how the whole day DC died played out. By trying to authentically retell that scene, it was like I traveled back in time and felt my loss on a deep, immediate level again.

It was also that way with my first dog. When I lost Winnie, my red Doberman rescue, I missed her so much. My eyes would well up when I thought about her. Enter my current dog Missie. She is a bounding ball of joy. Not a replacement for my departed dog, but a sweet companion who keeps me "in the moment."

Should I See a Therapist?

A possible indicator that it might be wise to seek professional counseling in order to work through the loss of a horse is when grief is impairing your life. If you find you are struggling to function at work or in your personal life, a trip to the therapist's office could greatly benefit you.

In the United States, when psychologists earn their degree, the subject of pet loss is briefly addressed. According to Dana White, a Southern California based LMFT (licensed marriage and family therapist), "My graduate program included one grief and loss class. We did discuss the loss of a pet as the loss of a family member. However, there was no curriculum specifically for grieving the death of a pet. It would be valuable information for every therapist to have."

White offers the following advice. "There are therapists who specialize in grief and loss. When searching for a therapist, ask if he or she has additional training or certification in grief and loss. If you are looking for a therapist through an online therapist listing service like psychologytoday.com, use the filtering option to select 'Grief' under the 'Issues' category. Also, David Kessler is an expert on grief and loss. His website, grief.com, is a good free resource for valuable articles and videos."

Each of us is unique, and no one will process grief in the exact formula laid out in the Kubler-Ross model: denial, anger, bargaining, depression and acceptance. For this reason, I believe that some horse lovers might benefit from sharing their loss with a professional counselor— someone who has been trained to listen well and ask good questions that help guide the bereaved toward emotional health.

Regarding Pet Grief Counselors

If you do plan to go down the route of seeking professional counseling, vet your counselor as you would any horse during a pre-purchase exam. It's easy to create a website and sell services to people, so if you conduct an online search for a pet grief counselor, make sure the person is well trained to assist you.

For example, I came across a website after doing some Googling and a person was selling services for grief counseling. This individual was not an actual licensed psychologist. The rate listed for one pet grief phone counseling session was higher than one month's board for my horse Knight! People who are grieving can be vulnerable, and it wasn't readily apparent whether this person was indeed a qualified counselor to pour your heart and pocketbook out to.

Find Comfort in Faith

As I mentioned earlier, I'm a Christian, and my faith is important to me. I know there is no biblical evidence that animals go to heaven. However, I also know that the Scriptures teach "His eye is on the sparrow."

If a loving God cares about sparrows, wouldn't He also care about noble, beautiful horses? And surely He cares about the heartbroken horse mourner. The book of Revelation states that in the future, Jesus will ride on a white horse. Hmmm. . . isn't that evidence horses *are* in heaven?

Perhaps you are of a different religious tradition or not particularly religious. Yet maybe there is a spiritual truth or faith practice that would help you. In a book called *Mudhouse Sabbath,* the author Lauren Winner outlines Judaism's mourning path, which consists of a series of rituals over the course of a year. It's followed up with annual acknowledgments.

"This calendar of bereavement recognizes the slow way that mourning works, the long time it takes a grave to cool, slower and longer than our zip-zoom Internet-and-fast food society can easily accommodate. Long after your friends and acquaintances have stopped paying attention, after they have forgotten to ask how you are and pray for you and hold your hand, you are still in a place of ebbing sadness. Mourning plateaus gradually, and the diminishing intensity is both recognized and nurtured by the different spaces the Jewish mourning rituals create."

These following words really popped out at me and made me think of how contrary modern-day culture is. It seems those of us in the 21st century think faster is better in weighty matters of the heart. From the loss of a horse to the breakup of a relationship, it's best to "move on" and "get over it." The ancients took a much different approach to grieving and grief.

Dia de los Muertos

On the three-year anniversary of DC's death, I reflected on him again and the significance of Dia de los Muertos, a holiday I had heard of and noticed around Halloween time when skulls began popping up in the plant section at Trader Joe's. Because it was not part of the culture I grew up around in the Midwest, I wasn't familiar with what the holiday was all about. I gained a very basic understanding from teaching an ESL class at my church and hearing from several of the students. The following is a blog post I wrote in 2013.

Today is Dia de los Muertos, a holiday celebrated in Mexico and some cities in the U.S. with large Mexican-American populations. The literal translation of the holiday is "Day of the Dead." This day is set aside for the living to honor the memory of family and friends who have passed away.

Today is also the three-year anniversary of the death of my favorite, most beloved horse, DC.

I was at Little Wood Farm in the aisleway grooming another horse the first time I saw his elegant face with the striking, backward question mark blaze. His long neck hung out over the top of the stall door as he was nibbling on and tossing his nylon halter, which was hanging nearby on a hook.

I thought to myself, "That is the most beautiful horse I've ever seen."

Little did I know that several months later, the mischievous halter-chewer would be mine.

Last week while teaching my Thursday night ESL class of intermediate English-speakers, the subject of Dia de los Muertos popped up. I was surprised to learn that basically every culture besides the United States has an annual celebration that honors the deceased. Korean, Thai and Per-

sian cultures have similar celebrations to Day of the Dead which occur around their respective new year or spring.

My ESL students explained that in order to honor their loved ones who have passed away, it's common to place an item that represents the person at the table to serve as a reminder. For example, if great uncle liked to smoke a pipe, a pipe is placed at the table for the day.

In the United States we don't really have one day set aside every year to remember loved ones no longer with us. We have Memorial Day, but that holiday is focused mostly on those who've fallen in battle, not necessarily deceased family and friends. And, of course, there is no day set aside to commemorate the life of a family pet, let alone horse, that has passed away.

Regardless, today I remember.

DC was magnificent. He was the fulfillment of this horse-crazy girl's dreams. He was my best friend for 16 years.

DC was a stunning bay Kentucky Thoroughbred with the world's shortest, fuzziest forelock that contrasted with the longest, thickest black tail. In the spring before the sun faded his coat, he had brown dapples.

DC loved being photographed and would point his ears forward, taking on a very interested and intelligent expression. I think he knew just how handsome he was.

DC's canter was buoyant and expressive and

not the easiest to sit, yet so fun—better than any Disneyland ride.

DC was a blast, and frequently challenging in a keep-the-rider-on-her-toes kind of way.

Especially when he was young, DC would select a "scary corner" of pretty much every arena we rode in. It might be near a mounting block or by the far end of the outdoor arena, close to trees or maybe near a rail where someone temporarily draped a longeline or left a winter blanket. No matter how many days we'd ridden past the scary corner, he'd routinely spook, whether big (leaping away from the evil corner) or small (simply flinching his muscles and tensing) when faced with it again. I think it was an act.

One day when DC was around 10, I turned him out in the empty indoor arena so he could buck and thunder around, tiring himself out before my ride. He put on a brilliant display of racetrack speed and intensity, rocketing from one end of the arena to the other, narrowly missing jump standards in the middle.

As he huffed and puffed and raised his tail like an Arabian, he shot off directly toward the gate that separated the barn aisle from the indoor ring. I knew he couldn't stop in time and feared he would crash through the solid wooden gate.

I was wrong. He flew over the four-foot top rail. I watched in horror and awe. A few boarders in the aisle way with horses on cross-ties got quite a show, both with the impressive aerial escape and *me sprinting across the barn in chaps and paddock boots to capture my temporarily insane steed.*

Everyone loved my handsome gelding at the various barns where he was boarded in Illinois and California. He endeared himself to both family and friends. Even people who didn't know him would stop us at horse shows and start talking to me about my pretty bay.

I'll never forget one show several years ago. A woman approached me as I was hand-walking DC. She asked a series of questions ranging from how old he was to how long I'd had him to what I fed him. She concluded our chat by patting DC's forehead and instructing me, "Take good care of my boy."

I will honor my boy's memory today regardless of how silly it might seem to a non-horse person or how lame it might seem to someone who is not sentimental.

It is Dia de los Muertos today.

Tonight, there will be organic carrots with feathery stems and crisp green apples on a plate at my table, as I continue to miss him and remember.

If fox hunts host annual "Blessing of the Hounds" ceremonies in which a local priest says a prayer for horses and hounds, that proves it's absolutely not ridiculous to commemorate a dearly departed horse.

Chapter 4 "Embrace Your Grief" Optional Assignment

- Share the story of your horse and how much he or she meant to you with a few non-horse people.

- If you want a greater challenge, and you still haven't written the eulogy, read the eulogy I wrote for my horse DC in Appendix A, then go to the Horse Eulogy Template in Appendix B and write a eulogy for your horse.

Remember, if you feel you are struggling to function at work, school or in your personal life, consider seeking counseling from a licensed psychologist.

CHAPTER 5

Commemorate

I HAVE TWO beyond beautiful photographs of DC that capture his essence.

One is at my mom's house in Illinois, where DC gallops through her office, pure poetry in a pasture with blazing autumn trees in the background. His dark chocolate form barely touches the ground, hooves hovering over the earth. The second one is a portrait of DC and me—I am smiling and hugging him while his ears are pricked and head held high. I cherish this photograph of the two of us together, although I rarely view it.

Just as each person is unique with how he or she grieves, each person will have a way that is comfortable to commemorate a dearly departed horse. What works for me might not work for you and vice versa. This chapter offers a variety of ideas fellow equestrians have employed to honor the life of a special horse.

Photos to Have and to Hold

I don't have that picture of DC on display at my house

because I want to focus on the present. I don't cry like I did when my loss was fresh; however, that photo makes me nostalgic. When I gaze upon the image, I'm reminded of mortality—DC's and my own.

The photograph is of a much younger me in a turtleneck with windswept hair smiling and posing next to the world's most beautiful horse. The frame is as shiny and bright as I felt every time I sat on the back of DC. That one is here with me in California. As I type this, our horse and rider headshot is wrapped in packing paper, tucked into a Lululemon bag, hanging out in a cabinet in my dining room.

The special purpose that photo now owns is as part of my display when I do book signings, since so much of my story in *Horses Adored and Men Endured* revolves around DC being my constant when dating was a series of disappointments. Having his picture there is a way to showcase a bit of what that story is all about.

His Story Lingers

Other than my photos of DC, I feel like I commemorate him when I tell stories about him, whether in person or through my writing. Some of the finest memories of DC are found on the pages of my memoir. His memory will be kept alive as long as my book is available and in print or residing on fellow horse lovers' e-readers.

One of my favorite stories to tell is about the time he was basically a nightmare at a local schooling show I went to after I had not shown in several years.

I didn't have a trainer with me that day, and basically everything that could have gone wrong did go wrong, from not having all my necessary tack to DC getting loose and galloping around at the showgrounds and causing quite a stir. If you can envision a horse show black sheep, that was us. But in the end, when we were in the ring, he performed like a true gentleman, not the banshee that he had been all day long.

I also enjoy recounting the time he jumped out of the indoor arena in Illinois. By sharing these stories in verbal or written format, I glory in what was special about my heart horse. I still miss him, a decade after his departure, but I have mostly gratitude paired with a mild twinge of empty.

If you are a storyteller like me, maybe that will be the strongest way for you to remember your wonderful horse, but it's just one of several options.

Paintings

In addition to having beautiful photographs on display or simply to look at from time to time, another way to commemorate a special horse you've loved and lost is by commissioning a painting. There are artists who can create a beautiful likeness of your horse based on a photo reference, and there are varying styles/mediums and price points.

If you like bold colors and dramatic strokes, check out Kasia Bukowska Art. Kasia has an Etsy business and a dramatic story of learning how to paint while battling lupus and fibromyalgia. She frequently paints horses and dogs that are no longer with us.

Kasia says that generally a family member will reach out to her for the commission, and it's often around the three-month mark. She feels it's good to have a time gap after the loss so the picture is meaningful, not a fresh reminder.

Here is an insight into how the process of working with an artist to paint your special horse might go, based on how Kasia connected with one of her clients.

"The customer told me a bit about the horse's story, about his last days and wanted a painting with some color, but she felt so lost she didn't know exactly what picture or what color(s). Just that she wanted his portrait.

She sent me a bunch of pictures and I told her what I thought would be the best picture and why, knowing a bit about the horse's story. Greenish on the bottom symbolizing the horse's last years out in pasture and it blends into a yellowish-white, symbolizing his passing spirit toward the light into horsey heaven.

I chose a picture of her horse staring off into the distance so it would appear that he's looking toward the light. His pricked ears show he's not afraid and his spirit is peaceful. I related to the person's heartache, losing such a special horse."

I mentioned Kasia because I know her in real life and can vouch for her work. She has also experienced tragic loss of horses (one of them being a foal). However, there are countless equestrian artists all over the world who would love to paint a special commission that will honor your horse. It's important to choose one whose style of work you love and who you feel can translate the photos you have into a legacy work of art.

Plant a Tree

There's something very satisfying about planting a tree. Trees are beautiful, and they produce oxygen for us to breathe. They are required for life itself.

Trees provide shelter and shade for various creatures, horses and humans included. You can plant a tree in your yard at home, or if you have your own pasture, perhaps plant a tree in a special spot where your horse liked to hang out. I've heard of horse owners planting apple trees (presumably not in a pasture) as a means to remember a horse's favorite treat. I know of a woman who had a black pony for years and when he died, she found a tree that had very dark, almost black leaves and planted it in his honor.

If you don't have the space for a tree, a plant could work nicely too. When I was a girl and my grandfather died, someone gave my grandmother a Dieffenbachia house plant. Today, 40 years later, one of my cousins still has that original plant. It has produced shoots that were made into potted house plants for other family members and friends. That one plant has been meaningful to a number of people. And the memory of my grandfather lingers.

Ashes

If your horse has been cremated, you will have a significant volume of ashes to deal with. Some horse owners prefer to keep these in their homes as a way to have their horse be present. Keep in mind, horses are huge, and their ashes will be extremely heavy. I've heard of people keeping a small box or urn of ashes and then scattering the rest as a means to enrich the soil. If you do plant a tree, it will benefit from having the ashes near its base as nourishment.

It's up to your personal preference what to do with the ashes, and there is no single perfect answer. As with the grieving recommendation, do what feels right for you. I did not keep DC's ashes and I have no regrets.

Jewelry

Using a lock of tail braided into a bracelet has been a traditional way to keep a special horse close forever. Recently some more innovative jewelry items including earrings and necklaces that incorporate ashes have entered the scene, from studs and hoops to dangling mane and tail tassels. To see examples of unique jewelry made from horse hair or ashes, go to saddleseekshorse.com/commemorating-your-horse. I have created a page with resources related to commemorating a special horse.

Horseshoes and Shadow Boxes

If your horse wore shoes and you've kept them, they can be repurposed into meaningful keepsakes. Ideas abound on Pinterest, such as simply taking one shoe and having it framed (with or without glass), or making it into a picture frame. The possibilities are endless.

Shadow boxes are also popular, and one horseshoe or a whole set can be artfully laid out along with a halter, lock of tail, photos, horse show ribbons or even a bit. If you are not artsy-craftsy and don't want to take your items to a frame store to have the shadow box professionally designed, you can get an end table or coffee table to display your horse's special items.

If you would like to see examples of shadow box displays, you can visit my website at saddleseekshorse.com/commemorating-your-horse.

Trophies and Advertisements

If the horse you've loved and lost was a show horse, a meaningful way to remember him or her is to sponsor a perpetual trophy at a horse show that was significant to you and your horse. Reach out to the show organizers and see if they will make arrangements to allow you the honor of donating the trophy. You can have the trophy engraved with the show name of your horse and perhaps also a short, meaningful phrase next to the name.

Local or regional horse magazines are perfect mediums to publicly place a remembrance ad. The ad can be simple, with just a beautiful photograph or two and a short statement about your horse. I've seen them before in the format of the horse's show name, barn name, years lived, and then a phrase like, "Forever in our hearts."

Tattoos

If you are an equestrian open to tattoo art, consider a remembrance tattoo of your horse a way to stay connected permanently. A simple Google search of "horse remembrance tattoos" will yield scores of photos to give you inspiration. Some tattoos are simple, like the name of the horse and horse shoes. If your horse has a brand, you can take on the brand as your own. For an off-track Thoroughbred, you could use your horse's Jockey Club lip tattoo number. Wrists, ankles, shoulders and lower backs are popular locations for these tattoos.

If you want to be more elaborate, think about using a meaningful phrase along with your horse's name, such as "thunder is the sound of hoofbeats in heaven" or "lending me the wings I lack." For a more elaborate way to remember your horse, you could have a headshot or silhouette of your steed forever emblazoned on your body.

Donation to Veterinary Medicine or Equine Non-Profit

Consider making a charitable contribution to a university's veterinary medicine program. If your horse died from illness, it might make you feel a little bit lighter to write a check to a program that researches the particular condition your horse encountered.

For example, the University of California-Davis has a specific Equine Tribute Memorial Fund which goes to support clinical research studies sponsored by the Center for Equine Health. They also have an Equine "Pay it Forward" Fund which helps other horse owners who have brought their horse to the university's equine hospital pay their vet bills when they're in a time of need.

The Gluck Equine Research Center at the University of Kentucky is on the forefront of scientific discovery for the well-being of horses. Several faculty and staff specialize in studying infectious diseases of all varieties: viral, bacterial, and parasitic organisms that threaten horses throughout the world. A donation to The Gluck Equine Research Center will amplify health care options for horses far and wide.

Brooke USA is a wonderful non-profit that assists horses, donkeys and mules in the poorest areas of the world. The organization was founded in the 1930s by Dorothy Brooke, and it initially set out to relieve the stress and suffering of horse veterans from World War I who had been left in Egypt. A British woman in Egypt over a decade after the war, Dorothy was appalled at the desperate conditions of animals who had served their country valiantly in battle. She wrote a letter to a newspaper that later became London's *Daily Telegraph* to raise awareness of the plight of the horses.

By supporting Brooke, you will bring hope to hard-working horses and their owners who rely on their animals for their livelihood. The main office for Brooke is in London, but they have a branch in the U.S. in Lexington, Kentucky.

There are countless horse rescues both large and small around the country that would benefit from a memorial donation. Perhaps the most fitting way to contribute is by finding a local rescue to partner with as a way to remember your horse.

Custom Model Horses

If you would like a small-scale replica of your special horse, there are Etsy artists who can paint a Breyer model to look just like him, right down to the dapples or snip on their muzzle. Visit saddleseekshorse.com/commemorating-your-horse for more information and links if you would like to have a model horse to remind you of your beloved horse.

Commemorative Donating of Your Horse's Possessions

One last question remains: what do I do with all my horse's things?

From fly sheets to saddle pads and beyond, the amount of horse stuff we accumulate over the years can be overwhelming. If you plan to get another horse down the road, go ahead and store your items. Keep in mind, however, when you do get a new horse, needs and sizes may change, plus it's fun to buy new.

Here's my story of what happened with DC's Baker Blanket. I had a hard time letting the classic plaid blanket go, even though it had been eight years and didn't fit my new horse Knight. The following piece first appeared on my blog Saddle Seeks Horse.

Love, Loss and a Baker Blanket

The skies were deceptively blue on Saturday as several wildfires continued to rage across Southern California. I had been in a gloomy mood most of the week, feeling sad and helpless as I scrolled through social media seeing reports of the losses of barns and horses. The scenes of orange-gray skies from the Lilac, Thomas, Creek, Rye, Skirball and Liberty Fires hit a little close to home. I'm technically a wildfire victim myself.

Victim seems like such a strong word.

Wildfire-affected?

Maybe that's a better term. [My horse's barn burned in Canyon Fire 2 in 2017. We were about nine weeks into our temporary relocation at the time of this writing.]

I had to do something to help and maybe ease my own sadness, but I couldn't think of what to do.

I know how to write, but all the writing about the fires was being handled by journalists.

I wasn't that close to the fires, so I couldn't really find someone to interview to share a first-hand account on this blog.

I have a day job and didn't feel right about calling in sick to go fill water buckets or blanket horses at one of the many evacuation locations in the southern part of my state.

I wanted to feel part of a community. I wanted to make a difference. I wanted to help ease someone else's pain, if just a little bit.

That Friday night, I had a burst of inspiration: I realized I could give away lots of the things I still had after "our" fire!

I PLACED MY Baker blanket, still fresh from its spring cleaning, folded neatly in a plastic bag, on the table designated for donations for fire victims.

"I can't remember the last time I used a cooler," I said

to the two volunteers at the table as I kept carrying armfuls of goods over from my car.

"The Baker was my previous horse's. It doesn't fit my current horse that well, and we got donations. We were in the October fires and lost our barn, so he has a new blanket." I started to choke up.

"You don't have to give that away," said one of my barn friends in a sweet tone. I didn't realize she was standing there as I made my donations.

"Yes, I do."

My friend looked at the ladies accepting donations at the horse show booth at the Los Angeles Equestrian Center and said, "It was her heart horse's blanket."

I sniffed and turned to hug my friend, tears filling my eyes. She said, "But you have Knight now," as she hugged me back.

The kind woman at the donation drop off asked me

the name of my horse that had owned the blanket.

"DC."

Her eyes looked a little red and she told me she had a Baker blanket from a favorite horse who was no longer alive. "They just last," she said, talking about the durability of the Baker brand.

"I'm going to make sure that this blanket goes to a special horse. Was DC a Thoroughbred?" At that point I couldn't talk, so I nodded.

I took a deep breath and somehow rattled off, "Kentucky-bred but never raced. Lived in Illinois and moved with me here to California. Bay with a blaze."

"I'm going to give this to the right horse. I'll make sure it's a Thoroughbred."

AT THE TIME of this writing, I heard there were 900 evacuated horses staying at Del Mar Racecourse. Really any horse who needed a blanket and was about 16 hands, Thoroughbred or not, would be the right horse.

It was through this conversation with the two angels accepting physical donations that I found out about the two hundred or so hot walkers and grooms from the racehorse training facility, San Luis Rey Downs, who had lost everything.

They worked to save as many horses as they could, but their living quarters and possessions are now ash.

"They were sleeping on concrete at Del Mar last night." My heart broke. I wished I had my blow-up *mattress from home, extra comforters, or a sleeping bag with me. I would have added those to my pile, which contained two coolers, two girths, a scrim sheet, anti-sweat sheet, a plastic tub with saddle pads and polo wraps and a bridle cleaning hook along with a pair of paddock boots that were just a little too big for me.*

About the same time another person came over to our donation corner. "Here are riding clothes. There's a really beautiful dressage show coat in here." She unzipped a garment bag to reveal the jacket.

I felt sad for myself because we lost our barn. This woman had lost her home and her horse's home. How unbearable.

At that point, I thought of one other thing I had in my car—actually two! I'd accidentally brought home and had with me a pair of nice Roeckl riding gloves. I have three pairs! I can only ride with one pair. Maybe someone else who lost everything would be encouraged by having a pair of almost-new riding gloves.

Yes, insurance will probably cover most people, but having to wait to buy new gloves would be inconvenient. And some people might not want to file claims—people like me.

My insurance company said they'd raise my rates 45% for the next three years if I filed a claim. At that point, it didn't seem in my financial best interest to claim my Canyon Fire 2 losses, so I was out several thousand dollars. Maybe there was someone else in my same situation—not wanting to file a claim and then incur an astronomical increase to their homeowner's policy.

I walked back over to the plastic bin, unsnapped the

blue lid on one side and tucked the gloves inside. I felt
really good. I helped.

In the scheme of all the loss, my contribution was
small, but it might give another rider or horse lover some
hope. Maybe the tiny, vintage Christmas card I shoved
into the bottom of the right paddock boot with the note,
"I'm praying for you, and I know what it's like to be
affected by a barn fire," would lift a fellow horse lover's
spirits.

It became really clear to me after the October fire in
which our horses were safe but the barn burned: All a
horse girl really needs is a saddle, bridle, saddle pad and a
girth. And a helmet, hoof pick and a couple of brushes.
That's really it. If you're younger and a more highly
skilled rider than me, the saddle and bridle might even be
optional.

As I turned to leave, the quieter one of the donation
coordinators approached me. "I have a 31-year-old
OTTB. I understand."

She knew why giving up a blanket would make me
cry, and why I had to do it.

The tender responses from the three women—one
friend and two Thoroughbred-loving strangers who "got
me"—as I gave away a piece of my heart in Baker blanket
form was a gift I will hold on to.

Chapter 5 "Commemorate" Optional Assignment

- Select a handful of items your horse used that you no longer need and donate them to a local horse rescue. Start with simple things like brushes. Your next horse will be worthy of getting his own new brushes!

- If you want a greater challenge, choose one way to commemorate your horse, whether through commissioned artwork or creating a shadow box filled with mementos that best represent your relationship.

- For more ideas on how to celebrate the life of your horse, visit saddleseekshorse.com/commemorating-your-horse.

CHAPTER 6

Attempt the New

WHEN DC DIED it was the end of an era.

I knew that I would have another horse one day, but that day sure didn't seem soon. You see, a few months earlier, teachers in California were pink slipped, and my school district actually delivered a pay decrease for that school year in order to avoid having to let teachers go.

On top of that, my new husband and I had purchased a home that was very nice—in 1979. We had a ton of remodeling and upgrades to do, like pouring concrete over the in-house dirt floor next to the kitchen that had been an "atrium."

Overwhelmed by a grimy fixer of a house coupled with a pay decrease and the lack of a nearby place to board, horses were temporarily on hold.

What Do I Do Without My Horse?

During that time, I got more interested in gardening and composting. I can't explain the satisfaction of taking coffee grounds, celery stems, egg shells, and apple cores and having them morph into sweet-smelling, dark brown compost, but it's real.

Also in the realm of gardening, during my horse dry spell my neighbor introduced me to the joy of succulents. I will never forget her snapping off a green aeonium and handing it to me with its thick rootless stem, looking like a stick. She told me all I had to do was shove the succulent in soil and it would grow.

She was right.

Today I have hundreds of succulents from her first sharing of the plants.

These new pursuits did not at all replace my horse love, but they gave me another outlet.

I also volunteered teaching English as a Second Language at my church. I actually met a few other women who loved horses; we went on a trail ride on rental horses up to the Hollywood sign and then had tacos at a Mexican restaurant right outside the Los Angeles Equestrian Center.

It wasn't the same as having my own horse, but it gave me hope that I could still find other horse lovers, and it helped tide me over until I could go full-force into riding and horse shopping again.

I also started taking a class called Body Pump at the gym. I'll never be buff, but I feel good about lifting weights, which is good for bone health. Doing squats and push-ups translates well into being strong for riding. I began attending spin classes. I went to a handful of cooking classes. I sharpened my meal prep and knife skills literally and figuratively.

Outside of the realm of horses, there are a whole host of wonderful pastimes. I had been a lindy hopper for several years before DC died, but after he was gone, I was able to get more involved in dancing pursuits. I started attending more swing dance camps and workshops. They're really fun. Not on the same level as riding fun—never a replacement hobby—but fun nonetheless. And good exercise!

None of the new things I attempted captured my heart the way horses had decades earlier, but I valued the enrichment. Learning is great for brain health, so all of those outside activities were good for me, even as a non-riding equestrian.

My sister told me a story about the time she bumped into tennis great Chrissie Evert at a tennis tournament my teenage niece was playing in several years ago. Chrissie was impressed by my niece and paid a compliment about her ability. My sister sheepishly told Chrissie that her daughter was playing tennis, volleyball and doing other enrichment classes on the side. Chrissie affirmed her by saying it's good for kids to try all kinds of activities and be involved trying different things. That was not what my sister expected to hear!

We can extend Chrissie's same logic over to adult equestrians. Riding is phenomenal, but so are other activities and pastimes. Really, if you think about it, any form of exercise or intellectual enrichment will hone our riding and empathy skills, making us better for horses.

Chapter 6 "Attempt the New" Optional Assignment

- What is one activity you have always wanted to try, even if just one time, but you never made it a priority because you had so much time invested in your horse? Schedule that thing.

- If you want a greater challenge, pick a new recreational activity (such as dance class or a specific class at the gym) that will help you be a stronger, fitter rider when you're ready to return to the saddle (if you've taken a little break).

CHAPTER 7

Ride Again

AFTER DC DIED, I took an unintentional four-year break from horses. He died shortly after a major life change. I got married in July, and after an idyllic honeymoon to Turks and Caicos, I hit the ground running as a wife and new stepmom to two adolescents. The home we bought was the absolute worst house on the best street we could afford in Orange County (not easy on two teachers' salaries!).

I kept trying to find a place to board DC near where I lived and came up short, so I thought it was better for him to stay in Illinois as an old man horse, rather than force a new "city-horse" lifestyle on him. I didn't think it would be fair to take him from being outside in a huge dry lot with two friends all day and a stall at night to just a stall with no turnout.

DC had lived all his prior years with access to turnout. As glamorous as the reality shows featuring Orange County try to make it look, it's not remotely desirable for a natural type of horsekeeping.

I tried diligently to connect with people in a nearby equestrian neighborhood where I thought there might be someone who had a horse property with a small field—a place I could in good conscience board my senior horse. I was overwhelmed geographically and working a full-time job that required an hour-long commute.

A new barn for DC in California did not materialize.

One of the first times I rode after the loss of my horse was when my niece's friend's mom let me ride her Argentine polo ponies. Somewhere on YouTube is a very funny/embarrassing video of my first attempt at polo—I don't dare link to it! Let's just say for someone who knows how to ride all the gaits and jump, I felt like a newbie when I had the mallet in my right hand.

I was so tentative, horrified at the thought of possibly hitting the horse with the cumbersome, new-to-me stick! But that short time in the saddle gave me hope of a future with horses again. Even though I was trying out a new discipline for 30 minutes, that same joy of being in the saddle surfaced.

A year or two after that I visited my former trainer in Illinois, who also happens to be a dear friend. She forced me to hop on one of her horses. I was really nervous, but when I was in that borrowed saddle in a borrowed helmet and just jeans, I felt like I had come home again. I think that short ride set me on the path to knowing it was time to return to my passion. And for that I am grateful.

I resumed my search for an Orange County barn and called around to try to find a trainer with a lesson program so I could re-enter the horse world. It took several phone calls and a few trips in person. It was actually very discouraging because I had no horsey connections in my new location.

I received one returned phone call and went out to take a riding lesson with this new trainer. I told her at the outset that I wanted to start taking regular lessons and would soon be looking to buy a new horse. Four years was too long to be horseless!

As much as I enjoyed reactivating all those riding-specific muscles and taking in the smell of hay and sweet horse breath, the quest for my next horse was anything but fun.

Horses available in Southern California in my price range were either very young and green or older with health issues. I spent hours poring over online horse listings and checking everything from Craigslist to dreamhorse.com. I tried four or five horses and kept coming up dry.

I was really down, so I reached out to a friend who knew DC and me. She gave me the name of a farm that specializes in taking Thoroughbreds off the track to turn them into riding horses. When I called the owner and rattled off my bio and the qualities I was looking for in my next horse, she said she had a horse that fit that description and asked for my email.

The day I met this horse via email, I fell in love with him. Once I had swung my leg over the saddle and settled in for my ride, I had a sixth sense that this pretty bay gelding was the one for me. And that's how I met my handsome Knight. You can read dozens of stories about our ups and downs on my blog Saddle Seeks Horse.

In the years I've been with Knight, my heart has been full again. I still think about DC and remember how much I loved him. But in keeping with my hope to be present in the here and now, I lavish my affection and carrots on Knight. He humors me and plays along.

Is Knight my heart horse too? It's hard to say, but I am thrilled when he comes to me in the field, stands patiently while tacking up, and is a good boy 99% of the time when I ride. We haven't had the same length of time together yet that DC and I shared, but each day I get to be with him is a gift. Every ride is a slice of joy—he's really working me. And for that I am grateful.

Chapter 7 "Ride Again" Optional Assignment

- You know what to do. Get on out there and ride a horse. Any horse will do! Go have fun.

PART TWO
Interviews with Fellow Horse Lovers

CHAPTER 8

Losing a Heart Horse

Lauren Maas is a recent graduate from UC Davis and volunteer at CANTER California, a non-profit specializing in retraining and rehoming retired Thoroughbred race horses. It was there she met and fell for her current horse Gallon (follow Lauren and Gallon on Instagram at @equineendeavor). Her handsome bay gelding had pretty big horse shoes to fill, as he was the successor to Lauren's first love and heart horse Dante. Read about Lauren's process of doing right by her horse in his time of need.

DANTE WAS A 1995 American Warmblood gelding (Hanoverian x Thoroughbred/Appaloosa). He was my first horse, who my parents purchased for me when I was 12 years old in 2008. He was, in every way, my life's dream realized.

Dante taught me much of what I know about riding, was my mount at many horse shows, and carried me proudly through middle school and high school. My mom used to drop me off at the barn and I would spend hours playing with him in his paddock, taking pictures of him (or "selfies" of us) with my pink Nikon Coolpix camera (cell phones weren't a thing really). We did everything together.

When it came time for me to choose which college to attend, being from Sacramento, it was an easy choice: UC Davis. Not only did it have a great program for somebody aspiring to be a veterinarian, it also had an equestrian center on campus where Dante could live.

Two weeks after I began college in the fall of 2014, Dante broke his right hind leg. My vet warned that without surgery, it was very likely we would need to euthanize Dante. I felt very strongly that it was not Dante's "time" quite yet. He was only 19 after all, and I had made him promise to me he would see me through my undergraduate studies at Davis.

I spent endless hours at the barn, neglecting my studies, in order to make sure Dante would make it through his injury. He began getting stronger, and was eventually deemed "pasture sound," although he was to never be ridden again. I was paying for Dante myself at this point and worked two to three jobs at a time throughout my entire career at UC Davis in order to make sure I could provide everything Dante needed in order to stay comfortable.

Dante's chronic pain increased over the years, despite my best efforts to provide him with deep bedding, vet care and the best supplements on the market. He got to the point where he was no longer comfortable enough to lay down to sleep. He was diagnosed by his veterinarian with sleep deprivation, and we started him on another medication to help manage his chronic pain.

In late 2017, Dante ended up with cellulitis in his left hind leg, which was previously his "good" hind leg. He had numerous veterinary visits, antibiotics given, and stack wraps on his leg. We would get it under control and then it would flare up again. When it was flared up, he would not put weight on his left hind leg and began putting all of his weight on the right hind, the leg he had previously broken.

While trying to mend his left hind, his right hind began giving out. I watched one night as he laid down and failed several times to get back up before he finally did. When he was standing, his right hind would tremble. He was tired. I felt helpless.

I had a difficult decision to make, but after watching Dante decline rapidly those last few months, I decided it was time for Dante to no longer suffer in order to stay here with me. It was selfish for me to ask that of him.

On December 26th, 2017, I walked Dante from the UC Davis Equestrian Center across the street to the UC Davis Veterinary Medical Teaching Hospital for his euthanasia appointment. The entire time we walked, I thought, "I could cancel this appointment right now and we would have more time together," but I ultimately didn't, because I knew that I was doing what was right for him, which is what I always tried to do.

How would you characterize your grieving process?

I needed a very long time to process what had actually happened. Why did Dante die? I had so many questions. He was only 22, which in my opinion was way too young. I would have breakdowns and just lay in bed and cry. I already had photographs of him all over my apartment, but I put up even more, had canvases made, a Breyer made, and hung up his leather halter. I talked about it a lot to my family and friends, and cried each time I talked about it. Then I wrote about it. I still write about it a lot. I find myself reflecting on the day I said goodbye very frequently, remembering different details all the time. Most recently, I remembered the last words I said to him. I have also found a lot of continued inspiration from Dante, and feel that he still touches my life every day, which has made things easier for me.

Was there anything said to you that was comforting? Anything said to you that was not comforting?

The least comforting thing possible? "I know how you feel" or "when I lost my horse _____, I felt the same way" or "I totally understand girl."

The most comforting? A friend from England wrote to me and said, "Your love for that horse resonates across the seas." I will never forget her saying that to me.

What helped you heal? Were there certain actions you took that eased the pain?

Writing has definitely helped me heal by being able to

share my story. Being able to keep Dante alive by talking about him is so therapeutic for me. I have also been wearing a bracelet that says "Dante" on it for the past decade, and whenever I need some faith or strength, I rub my fingers over it. Feeling like he is still here helping to guide my life helps me an incredible amount.

I hope to open a non-profit to benefit senior horses in the future and call it Against the Wind Farms after Dante—Against the Wind was his show name. That's my biggest Dante-related dream, but I hope it happens someday.

What did you learn from losing a horse that you believe would help another person in the same situation?

That it's okay to say goodbye when the time is right for your horse, even if it doesn't feel right for you. I believe that euthanasia is a gift we are able to give to our animals, to end their suffering in a dignified and peaceful way, filled with love and good intention. This goes for horses with slow declining health like Dante, but also for horses who colic or who have had a traumatic injury where a decision needs to be made.

What else would you like fellow horse lovers to know?

My hope for everyone that has lost a horse is that they feel comfortable enough to share their story and talk about it. It's something I don't think we talk about enough.

CHAPTER 9

Losing a Childhood Pony

Laurie Berglie is a passionate horse lover and the woman behind the wildly successful and beautiful Instagram account Maryland Equestrian. Laurie has penned three equestrian romances: Where the Bluegrass Grows, Kicking On, and Taking Off (available on Amazon), and is a writer for the equestrian lifestyle magazine Horse and Style.

TAKOMA STAR WAS a bright bay Mustang who was born in Arizona. She was rounded up and adopted at the age of three. My parents bought her for me when I was 11; Takoma was 12, and I believe I was her third owner.

She was 14 hands and an all-around perfect first pony and friend. While she was kind of standoffish, she was gentle and very tolerant of me and my constant need to groom, pet and kiss her all the time. I was lucky enough to have her in our backyard on our small farm, so she was my constant companion. She went English and western, was the best trail horse, and an excellent show pony (4H and local hunter shows).

When she was in her late 20s, she was diagnosed with Cushing's disease, which didn't affect her too much in general. Other than not shedding her winter coat (we had to have her full-body clipped twice a year), she was a normal, healthy horse. The last two years of her life, it was difficult keeping weight on her—her teeth weren't great by then—so she received grain three times a day. I worked with an equine nutritionist to develop a plan that worked for her. She got breakfast, dinner, and what I called a "midnight snack"—grain around 9 or 10 p.m.

The night before we had to have her put down, she was completely normal. The following morning, she ate her breakfast just fine, but was favoring her right hind. I thought maybe she was abscessing, but just to be sure, I called my vet. I told her it wasn't an emergency, but I would like to have Takoma seen that day. I went back out to check on her about an hour later and could tell she was really struggling with her hind end. She was losing complete control of it. I called the vet and told her that it was an emergency after all, and she said she'd be there within a half hour.

Just before the vet arrived, Takoma went down and couldn't get back up. I sat with her and tried to soothe her. She was breathing heavily but didn't try to get up. My vet did a quick exam, determined there were no present injuries like a broken leg or back, and that she was most likely suffering from something related to the Cushing's disease. We chose to immediately euthanize her.

On December 5, 2017, a long and very beautiful chapter of my life came to a close. I said goodbye to Takoma Star. She was 36 years old.

How would you characterize your grieving process?

I had been preparing myself for this day for quite some time. When you have an animal that old, it's something you think about almost every single day. I thought grieving for her would be easier because all I had to do was think about the very long happy life she had, but it was much harder than I anticipated.

Any time an animal passes, they leave this gaping hole in your life, your heart, and your day. Walking into the barn and seeing Takoma's empty stall and her lonely halter, it was too much to bear. But I still had two other horses to take care of, so they were the perfect distraction. There are always stalls to be cleaned and hooves to be picked, so I couldn't sit inside and dwell.

Some days were easier than others, but that first month was rough. We ended up having Takoma buried on our property. A neighbor came with a backhoe later that evening and, with the help of my husband (I stayed inside), gave her a final resting place at the edge of their main dry lot. It was a place where she'd enjoyed standing and sunning herself.

One of the hardest things was watching my OTTB mare, Misty, grieve too, and it was a reminder that I wasn't the only one who was hurting. Misty and Takoma had been together since the day I brought Misty home nine years prior, and these two loved each other. Takoma took on a motherly role with Misty, who was only 4 when I got her. After Takoma passed, Misty would go out and lay on top of Takoma's grave. As you can imagine, that was heart wrenching. She did that regularly for about a month.

Was there anything people said to you that was comforting?

My family, friends, and neighbors all said similar things, reminding me what a good long life she'd had. My horse friends who had known Takoma almost as long as I had recounted their fun memories with her, and it made me happy to know she'd had a positive impact on so many. One of my favorites was when my best friend showed Takoma one summer. I grew to be rather tall, so I stopped showing Takoma toward the end of high school and instead rode my mom's Arabian gelding. Luckily I have always been slim, so I continued to ride Takoma until we retired her. My legs would hang down too long, but I was light enough for her to carry.

My best friend was a little shorter, so she decided to show Takoma that year. My favorite memory was when we were all in a walk/trot hunter class together. There must have been 15 competitors in the ring, all on large horses. And then there was Takoma, the cutest pony, just strutting her stuff. It was a local low-level show, but my friend braided Takoma's mane and tail anyway, and she was simply adorable. I was riding in the same class, but I remember trotting around and seeing Takoma just floating around perfectly, looking like the belle of the ball in her braids. We all lined up and the results were announced. Takoma took first place! She beat the pants off of a bunch of big, fancy horses. I was so happy you'd have thought I won!

What helped you heal? Were there certain actions you took that eased the pain?

Like I mentioned, we buried Takoma on our farm, so it makes me feel good that she's still here with us. I told my husband that we can never sell this place now! But it's nice to know that she's still here, and I talk to her sometimes too. I always tell her goodnight when I'm locking up the barn for the evening. I know she's still with me and watching out for Misty, especially, because Misty is silly and needs all the help she can get!

Other than sharing memories and looking at pictures, this poem was really comforting. Of course, we cut a chunk of Takoma's tail to save. It makes me happy to know that she's in horse heaven with part of her tail missing. Everyone can see that she was loved and indeed "did a very good job."

The best horses in Heaven
they have no tail.
This is a rule they all know
without fail.
For when a new horse arrives
with a short cut bob,
they all know that this horse
did a very good job.

His owner could not bear
to part with her friend
so she saved his tail,
wrapped in ribbons
and in braids,
to hold with his memory
in a very loving way.
To enter Heaven
without a tail
is an honor,
a message,
that without fail
announces to everyone,
far and wide
that this horse

was more than a wonderful ride.

But

this horse was loved and cherished by one
and when his time serving on this Earth was done

he left behind
a broken heart
and a soul
from which he never will part.

–Miska Paget

What did you learn from losing a horse that you believe would help another person in a similar situation?

I learned that losing a horse is completely different than losing a dog or cat. When my mom's best friend who also has horses found out I lost Takoma, she said, "When you lose a horse, you lose a life partner. A horse will walk beside you for 30 or more years. It's a lifelong love affair." That really stuck with me because it truly does seem like a lifetime. I was heading into 7th grade when I got Takoma; I was 35 when I let her go. She carried me through change after change, season after season. And while I encountered one new chapter after the next, she was my constant. She was and would always be the same. A link to my past, my childhood, a reminder of so much good.

I learned that horses really are partners. I don't know if we can ever completely "own" a horse the way we own dogs and cats. Dogs will love you no matter what, and of course there's nothing better than being greeted by a dog when you walk in the door. But a horse is a tremendously large animal who willingly allows us on their backs. To have the trust of a 1,200-pound animal is an incredible feeling, and the relationship that develops from this faith in one another is hard to describe. And once that partner is gone, it's quite simply devastating. It's okay to grieve for a horse the way you'd grieve for a longtime best friend.

I also learned that I needed to stay busy. And not just busy with work, but with horses. Even though being in the barn without Takoma was heartbreaking, being where she lived made me feel close to her. Yes, her little spark was gone, but the barn was still a happy place because of her. I ended up buying a farm four years before she passed, and it made me so happy to bring her home. I felt like things had come full circle. She was a backyard pony again, and I'm happy she got the retirement she deserved. I also like to think that she was proud of me. I had grown up before her eyes. But no matter where I went, so did she.

What else would you like fellow horse lovers to know?

I had a friend who lost her young horse very unexpectedly, and it was so traumatic for her that she got out of horses altogether. I know that everyone grieves differently, but I truly feel that her horse who died would not have wanted that. Her horse would have wanted her to find another to love and care for, to give another a wonderful home. Let a new horse be your old horse's legacy. You aren't replacing your beloved friend. Not in the slightest. Of course, take all the time you need, but I believe our horses would want to pay it forward, for us to find another friend, bring them into our lives, and start another lifelong partnership.

CHAPTER 10

Losing a Horse Unexpectedly

Amy Tomasheski is a long-time friend I first met when we boarded horses together about 25 years ago. When I was at the peak of showing my heart horse DC, Amy owned a fantastic Quarter Horse named Spud who was the kind of horse that made you feel like you could do anything. He was safe, steady, game and extremely cute. He jumped like a dream and was an all-around solid citizen. Every horse lover deserves to own such an amazing partner at least once in his or her life. Tragedy struck one day out of the blue, and Spud's life was cut way too short.

I GOT SPUD when I was 12 years old. He was my "first horse," not counting my pony Lassie. He was a registered chocolate palomino American Quarter Horse and built like the classic, old-school Quarter Horses from way back when. What's the most logical thing to do with a horse that was a Congress Champion? Turn him into a hunter, of course. That's what I did, and he was fantastic! Spud was the center of my childhood equine life.

I went off to college in the summer of 1993 and Spud stayed at home. I was home for summer in 1994. One afternoon I was home and Joanne, my trainer, called to say Spud was hurt in the pasture, and the vet was on the way, and to get out ASAP. We got there, and Spud was in the field standing on three legs with his right hind leg shattered.

I remember seeing it sort of flopping, but there wasn't really any blood. In Spud fashion, he stood like a champ. Dr. Heinze, my veterinarian, came out and Spud was too far into the pasture to get the x-ray out there. By that time, Spud had just laid down. He had been standing a while. I sat right down next to him. My friend Stephanie who was there later told me I sat down in a big fresh pile of poop, but I didn't notice.

Dr. Heinze splinted his leg, we got him up, and he walked straight into the trailer. I rode in the truck with my trainer and her husband and someone else (I can't remember who) rode in the back with Spud to keep him up as we drove to the clinic. I was sort of in a daze at this point. This was my first experience with this kind of emergency. I was scared, but in my mind, Spud was going to be okay.

Spud was propped up in a support stall and they took x-rays. The films were awful. His leg was shattered. I remember everyone not wanting to tell me the truth, but I just knew it was bad. I forced my trainer's husband to tell me. At that point I'm pretty sure I lost it. I don't remember everything, but I do remember crying and running out of the clinic to the parking lot. My two friends Stephanie and Liz followed me. They just held me.

I eventually went back in and begged Dr. Heinze to fix him. The 19-year-old me didn't think about anything other than saving him. Now as a 43-year-old, I probably would have had a similar reaction, but I more logically understand the reality of Spud's chances. When I was a kid, I had no idea.

The decision was made. My mom and I left before it was done. I was a disaster. I don't remember much of the next few days other than not wanting to ride. Spud was 14 when he died.

Flash forward several years, and my next horse Manny was my impulse purchase after a painful divorce. People used to ask me, "Why did you buy a horse?" and I would say, "Because I can," so that became the name I showed Manny under.

He was a 16-year-old registered Appaloosa, with that classic Appy personality. Sweet, with just a dash of stinker thrown in. Not to mention stubborn. Manny was the start of my adult equine life. I rode between Spud and Manny—after all, it was a 20-plus year gap—but he was the first horse I owned all by myself. We had a grand old time.

We did some shows, but I mostly just loved on him and enjoyed him. I got Manny at the start of his senior years from a woman who loved him but didn't do much with him. I always said I wanted to retire Manny because I never got to retire Spud. I was able to do that for Manny.

The last three years or so of Manny's life were retirement. I rode him lightly, and he spent the majority of his time in turnout with Farris, a retired OTTB and his best buddy.

Manny had a bit of a sensitive gut. The first time he colicked, he faked us all out. He started showing signs, the vet came out, gave him meds, we walked him, he pooped, and all seemed well. Ha! I was back out there in the middle of the night and after two hours of trying—I told you he was stubborn—we got him into the trailer and were on our way to the clinic.

They hooked him up to IV fluids. We played the waiting game, and all was well about $3,000 later, but he was okay. He spent the weekend at the clinic and came home that Monday.

After that, he started getting extra gut supplements. We had three more incidents like that, but we knew he was a faker, so we didn't wait and see, we immediately oiled him each time. All three times, things resolved easily and were relatively mild. The last time was just before Halloween 2016.

I got a text around 8:30 a.m. on a Saturday. In my mind, I thought it was like the others. My regular vet was out of town, so my backup vet came out. I walked him, but Manny was a lot less cooperative this time. He seemed to be in more pain. Here's the thing about Manny: he was a lightweight when it came to pain. The vet came out and tried to do a rectal palpation to check for impaction, but couldn't get her arm in past her forearm. She couldn't tell what it was. By this time his gut was starting to look distended. She did a quick test to see if his gut had busted, which it hadn't, so we loaded him up in the trailer and off we went, back to the clinic. He loaded like a champ, which will tell you how much pain he was in.

Before we left, the vet asked me what she should tell the clinic. She was calling to tell them we were on the way so we could get on the road. I said Manny could be treated, but no surgery. By the time we loaded him up, I had a feeling this was not going to be good. Manny was almost 24 years old, had a significant heart murmur, and this was his fourth colic. Surgery probably wasn't going to be a viable option. I didn't want to just give up, so I agreed to the clinic because I promised him that I would do whatever I could for him and always keep his best interests and quality of life in mind.

We got to the clinic. They managed to get him stable and tried a few different meds, but it was not looking good. The vets agreed it was worth giving him a chance, but surgery would not be a reasonable option. There wasn't anything else I could do at the clinic, so I decided to go home. Before I left, I signed the equine version of a Do Not Revive—I lived a solid 1.5 hours away and I didn't want him to suffer waiting for me to get back to the clinic.

I left with the barn manager who drove us. We got back, had some dinner and stopped at Starbucks for some gift cards for the vets. That's when the call came in from the clinic. Manny went downhill fast, and there was nothing else they could do. I told them I was on my way, and not to wait. I promised him I would never let him suffer for me. They said it would take some time to get everything ready, but they wouldn't wait.

The barn manager drove and we flew back to the clinic. I called my husband Brad to tell him, but he was on duty (he's a county sheriff's officer) and couldn't leave his shift. I then called my best friend Chelsey. She and I had been horsey friends for a long time and Manny was like her own horse. We both cried. By the time I got back to the clinic, he was gone, lying peacefully in the grass next to the clinic. The vets had just covered him with a sheet.

We talked, and they told me everything. I cried and hugged him. I clipped his forelock and tail. They pulled his shoes. I was sad, but I also felt a lot of peace. I kept my promise to him and in some way, to Spud. I did everything I could and always kept his best interests at the forefront. I went back to the barn and everyone at the farm cried with me. My friends called and texted. I did the typical Facebook post and watched the comments flood in. It was a much different experience this time than with Spud. I was wiser, but no less sad than when Spud died. I think that just comes with time. It's not something you can teach or learn. It's just a part of life you experience.

How would you characterize your grieving process?

I know everyone talks about the stages of grief, and I'm sure I experienced all of them, but I'm not sure if it was obvious to me at the time. I know that seems weird, but for instance, with Spud, I tried to bargain with everyone. I had what ifs, et cetera ... Manny was a lot different. I had been through it already, not just with Spud but a few dogs as well. If I went through all of the stages, I got to acceptance pretty quickly. I feel like I was pretty logical about it, but on the other hand, I was anything but logical. I had made the decision long ago what my limits were, so I think that helped me grieve as well.

When I was younger, I wallowed in my own feelings and doubt about everything. As I got older, life experience gave me perspective. I cried and felt the pain of not only losing Manny, but Spud as well. However, there was an overwhelming feeling of peace that I kept my promise to do what was best.

Was there anything said to you that was comforting? Anything said to you that was not comforting?

Please, don't say "time heals all wounds" or any other silly cliché. Those are not comforting. It's like saying the sky is blue. What was comforting was knowing that people loved Manny and Spud as much as I did and were just as sad as I was. I was not alone in my grief. Just being told they felt my pain was the best thing anyone could say.

What helped you heal? Were there certain actions you took that eased the pain?

I know I just said lay off the cliché's, but time, that's what helped. And having friends around that said, "Anything you want, I'll help. Come ride my horse, whenever you want." Telling me their stories of loss. Despite the obvious fact that I am not the first, last or only person to go through this, it helped so much.

The best thing was Chelsey coming to my house the next day and taking me to breakfast and then to her barn to see her horses. We just hung out and enjoyed the ponies. Being around the animals helped a lot. People who knew Manny in his younger days were there and they were sad too, but also happy that he had me.

What did you learn from losing a horse that you believe would help another person in the same situation?

Have a plan. Make the decision and decide your "limits" well before anything actually happens. An emergency situation is not always a good time to make a decision. I decided long ago that because of Manny's heart murmur and age, surgery was not going to be an option. I owed it to him to have that plan in place and to be mature enough to do everything I could to not make rash decisions in the heat of the moment. My desperation to save Spud made me beg for a surgery that would have had questionable results and recovery process that likely would have been torture on his body. When the time comes, it won't make it any less sad, but it will make it a lot less stressful because you are doing what you decided was best for your horse.

What else would you like fellow horse lovers to know?

Nothing can fully prepare you for the moment you have

to make a decision, or the moment you actually lose your horse. All of my experience and plans didn't make it any less sad, but that's okay. It's not supposed to be an easy decision; if love fixed everything, then horses would live forever. Make a plan. Make your plan known to others who can be sure your wishes are carried out. Be sad. It's okay. Tell the same story over and over again. Everything you're feeling is valid. Again, I know I said I don't like clichés, but life goes on, and you will find another horsey love.

Also, I 100% believe in "heart horses." I also believe that you can have as many "heart horses" as you want. Spud was, Manny was, and now Roo, my off-track Thoroughbred is. They are all my "heart horse." Every horse deserves to be a "heart horse."

CHAPTER 11

Losing a Foal

Stephanie from Tulsa, Oklahoma is an eventer, fox hunter, and self-proclaimed "reluctant dressage queen" living on a small farm with three horses, five cats, two dogs, and her husband. Stephanie's dreams for breeding her mare didn't turn out as she planned, but she is eager to share her experience in the hopes she can help another horse lover who has journeyed down a similar path. Stephanie blogs about her equestrian life at www.handgallop.com.

I'D HAD THE idea to breed my mare Gina for years before her foal Marrakesh was born. I bought Gina in 2011 as an event horse; over the years, she became my primary dressage and fox hunting horse.

Gina is a 1997 Thoroughbred mare who was entered into the Main Mare Book of the Oldenburg Registry North America/International Sporthorse Registry (ISR-Oldenburg NA) long before I laid eyes on her. She produced Oldenburg fillies for an Oklahoma breeder in

2001 and 2002 before being sold to a Tulsa-based hunter/jumper barn. A few years ago, I met a woman at a horse show who owned the 2002 filly. She had only positive things to say about the horse: how athletic, good-natured, and amateur-friendly she was.

I've always believed Gina is a quality mare. She has good conformation, a generally pleasant attitude, and beautiful gaits. She's a mare with traits worth passing along. I began searching for Oldenburg stallions in 2015 and eventually settled on Manhattan, a gray Oldenburg stallion standing at Avalon Equine in Oklahoma. He checked all the boxes: he was ISR-Oldenburg NA approved, had a reputation for producing amateur-friendly offspring, and had many offspring on the ground performing well in a variety of disciplines.

My goal was to produce a sound, athletic horse with a good mind. I planned to keep the foal for my own use as a multi-purpose horse; I event, fox hunt, and do dressage, and wanted to breed a horse that could do those things. It was also important to me that the foal be marketable in the event I could not keep it for its entire life.

I bred Gina for the first time in 2016, but she resorbed the embryo several weeks after breeding. I bred her again in 2017, and she successfully carried the fetus to term. Gina's frequent ultrasounds and check-ups with the reproduction vet always went well, but I began to worry when she went weeks past her due date. Friends, experienced breeders, and my vet assured me that this was not unusual.

My regular vet (who worked out of the same clinic as

the reproduction vet) performed an ultrasound one afternoon when she happened to be at my neighbor's barn. She caught a fleeting glimpse of a squirmy, horse-shaped blob and jokingly asked me, "Did you breed Gina to a pony?" I told her I hadn't, and she commented that the fetus seemed small. She assured me it was very active, which was a good sign, and told me that she might be wrong about the size—after all, she wasn't a reproduction specialist. The comment stuck with me, though, and I worried more.

One sunny summer morning, I woke up to a call from my good friend next door: "YOU HAVE A BABY!"

My husband and I rushed outside to greet the newest member of our family, a tiny chestnut colt who was damp with dew and birth fluids. Gina had given no indication of foaling when I'd checked on her late at night. She'd given birth to her colt in the middle of a hay pile in the paddock with her two herd mates looking on instead of in the carefully prepared and deeply bedded foaling stall I'd been maintaining for weeks.

She stood over her foal, nudging him and nickering at him. He seemed content to lay on the ground, sitting up in a dog-like fashion. Gina let us crowd around him and admire his pink nose and curving ears and tiny hooves. I called my vet to let her know about the event, and she emphasized that it was very important for me to observe and follow the "1-2-3" rule: the foal should stand within one hour, nurse within two, and the placenta should pass by hour three. Gina's placenta was already on the ground, but her colt still had the feathery looking eponychium on his hooves. He had not been up very much since birth, if at all.

I was in constant contact with my vet throughout the morning. She advised us to help him up and gently position him towards Gina's udder. We did. He was painfully thin and extremely wobbly. He nursed but seemed exhausted by the process and laid back down quickly. We repeated the process a few more times while waiting for another vet from the clinic to come out and conducting a post-foaling exam on Gina and check out the foal.

The vet who came out was not my usual vet and was not familiar with my horses. He was an older man with years of experience with mares and foals, and he was clearly worried once he assessed the situation. Gina was in great shape—no tearing, no retained placenta, and plenty of milk. But the foal was in a bad way. He milked Gina so her colostrum wouldn't go to waste and advised me to get the foal to the clinic as soon as I could. I hooked up the truck to my trailer and loaded Gina and her foal with some assistance from my neighbor.

Over the next month, Gina and Marrakesh were in and out of the veterinary hospital. I'm fortunate to live fairly close to one of the top veterinary facilities in the state. My horses received excellent, round-the-clock care. Marrakesh initially received a feeding tube and IV of fluids. He rallied and was cleared to go home after about a week. At home, he developed a fever that wouldn't abate. He and Gina went back to the clinic, where he was diagnosed with an infection at the IV site. For the next few weeks, the vets struggled to combat the infection.

They were ultimately unsuccessful. The infection settled in his hock joint; the prognosis was so poor that I didn't hesitate to euthanize him. What kind of life could a completely crippled horse enjoy?

How would you characterize your grieving process?

My grieving process was relatively brief and intense. Marrakesh's death was upsetting; he had a tragically short life full of suffering. For a few weeks, I felt disappointment, sadness, and guilt. My dreams of competing on my own homebred horse died. I felt foolish and questioned why I'd thought I was knowledgeable and experienced enough to breed my mare. I owed the vet a staggering amount of money that far exceeded the sum I'd saved up for foaling expenses. Most of all, I felt guilty for bringing a life into the world only to suffer.

Those feelings eventually subsided. I knew the veterinary team did their very best for my foal and that I pursued every reasonable treatment. They treated him with kindness and affection. He'd always been with his mother. He enjoyed a few days galloping around my paddock like a typical foal. And he passed peacefully.

I spent the next couple of months feeling completely unmotivated to ride or do much of anything with my horses. I was emotionally exhausted and couldn't muster up the enthusiasm to work with my green horse or even trail ride on my old horse. That depression also abated. While I still feel sad when I think of Marrakesh, I don't dwell on his death and can again enjoy my horses who are still here.

Have you lost an older horse? If so, in what way was losing your foal different from a previous horse?

Several years ago, I lost an older horse named Jethro. I was on vacation in Colorado at the time and received a call from my dad. He'd found Jethro in the pasture, dead. I was stunned, as Jethro was only in his teens and appeared to be in good health.

Losing Marrakesh was more painful. I felt responsible for his life and his death. He was also a horse I'd pinned many hopes and dreams to.

Was there anything said to you that was comforting? Anything said to you that was not comforting?

My friends and family were very supportive and kind. Most of them simply offered their condolences. Several horse bloggers and real-life friends also put together a sizable donation towards my vet bill, which I sincerely appreciated. My local friends helped take care of my other horses, helped me load Gina and Marrakesh in and out of the trailer, and took me on trail rides to keep me from spending all of my time worried and alone.

My vet joked that if I'd bred Gina to some hideous stallion and turned her loose in a pasture full of barbed wire and rusty car parts that she and Marrakesh would have turned out just fine. It was a relief to hear something humorous in the middle of this awful ordeal.

A few people tried to reassure me that at least Marrakesh knew he was loved; this wasn't a very helpful comment, as I did not share that sentiment. How could he know that, when most of his short life was spent in a vet hospital? I wasn't angry or very upset by these comments, though—I know they came from a kind place.

What helped you heal? Were there certain actions you took that eased the pain?

I didn't do anything in particular to heal. The passage of time was what helped the most. I took some time off from riding, though I couldn't avoid my horses entirely. They live with me, so I still had to care for them even when I was feeling sad.

What did you learn from losing a foal that you believe would help another person in the same situation?

I learned that it is very helpful to plan for the worst-case scenario, emotionally and financially. I didn't. I assumed that everything would progress normally and would turn out fine. There was no real reason to think it wouldn't, but if I'd planned for the worst-case, I would have had more savings to draw from and perhaps the hurt would have been a little less.

This experience also reinforced my practice of gratitude. I usually try to focus on the positives in any situation; it was hard to do with a dead foal and massive vet bill. But I was (and am) grateful that my mare Gina is healthy and well, that my friends were so generous with their time and money, and that I am not so broken-hearted that I cannot enjoy horses any more.

CHAPTER 12

Death of a Dream: When a Horse Requires Early Retirement

Melina is a lifelong horse lover from Florida who has garnered tens of thousands of social media fans on her Instagram account, @mpmsporthorses. Caraszini, a.k.a "Zini" or "the Rhino" is Melina's jumper she hoped to move up the ranks with and compete at the Grand Prix level. Zini's heart and personality are as big as the fences he jumped with gusto. In early 2019, Melina discovered Zini had a health issue that would drastically impact his future. Although he was and is still alive and well, a difficult decision was made to retire him. Melina's dream died and gave way to a new dream with her equine partner.

ZINI IS A 10-year-old KWPN Dutch Warmblood that I imported, sight unseen, from the Netherlands in 2016. I had never tried him, never got to see him in person. I was trying a horse in Nashville, a smallish and hot mare, and she didn't pass the pre-purchase exam. I remember the lady telling me, "If you like this one, I'm importing one in about a month. He's not on the market yet."

The seller showed me a picture and it was Zini. Her partner fell through on her half, and without her partner's financial contribution, she couldn't afford to bring him over to the U.S. I was the first one to make an offer. A sale barn got him because he was originally supposed to be a dressage horse, but he didn't thrive. Jumping was what he wanted to do. He was very green to the jumping side of things. When I saw his video, I knew there were definitely holes I could fill in if I put in the work.

The funny part is he really wasn't like the mare I tried out. He is 17 hands and super lazy. We all laughed when he came off the trailer.

What was your plot twist that changed his career?

I first noticed something different about Zini back in July of 2018. It was an on-and-off-again ordeal. We'd find something that seemed to be innocent and a simple fix. We'd X-ray, ultrasound, and examine him up and down. Usually we would only find something mild that could use injection. This led us to inject his stifles in August, hocks in September, and both sides of his sacroiliac joint in October.

Come November, I still didn't feel as if he was acting like his normal self, so I decided to have a full body bone scan/soft tissue scan and lameness location done. It was pretty inconclusive. I spent most of December desperate to find answers. In January I asked my vet to send in a referral for an MRI. My prayers were answered, and he was referred and scheduled for an MRI in February.

Despite suffering a severe complication from the anesthesia required for the MRI, we finally got our answer. Zini had a small birth defect in his left front foot. Because this defect is inoperable and not treatable, with the help of four independent veterinarians/specialists, I decided it was best that Zini retire from jumping. We'd been prepping to do the Grand Prix.

How would you characterize your grieving process regarding this death of a dream?

This is hard for me to explain. I was highly emotional, and it was almost as if my horse died that day. It sounds extreme, but that was the reality of it. I spent weeks crying. And although he was alive and well and still here with me, the part of him that I enjoyed the most was gone. I'd never get to feel him fly again. We would never reach our goals that we worked so hard for. We would never show or compete. It was all gone in an instant, overnight.

Was there anything said to you that was comforting? Anything said to you that was not comforting?

Everyone said so much, but none of it helped. I appreciated the gesture behind their words, they wanted to ease my pain, they wanted me to not feel so alone, but it didn't help. What stuck with me the most though was someone questioning my decision for his retirement. They told me I was pessimistic and "giving up on him" because of the decision I made for his best interest. It was not comforting, and it was quite hurtful. I thought the response would be a little more empathetic. It was like a jab into my gut. It came from the first person I told.

Also, it's not comforting when they ask about when you will get your next horse. People forget the simple things we should be grateful for. So many people want horses to be machines.

What helped you heal or what is still helping you heal? Were there certain actions you took/are taking to help ease the pain?

I think time can heal almost anything. There isn't a specific tool I have used that has helped heal my heart. There are still days that I see a photo, or someone sends me a sweet video they made, and I am sent instantly into tears. But I think learning to adjust to our new norm has helped. I may not get to tack up, go flat, go jump or train for a show in a lesson, but what's remained the same is my love for the animal. I can still enjoy spending time with him on the ground, being on his back on a trail ride, and coming to terms that THIS, this should be enough.

What did you learn from this type of loss that you believe would help another person in the same situation?

Time is not promised. Goals, dreams and aspirations don't always get fulfilled. But we can always turn a negative into something positive. This whole experience has opened my eyes and my heart to see my world in a whole new perspective. I still have so much to be grateful for. Zini is still here with me, he's alive and well. He has no idea why I don't put his saddle on, why we don't go school jumps, and he doesn't understand why I cry on his shoulder. But he understands my love for him. As a horse woman, you have to love your horse as a horse first and enjoy his job after that. Because if that job comes to an end, your horse still needs you there to love him.

What else would you like fellow horse lovers to know?

Everything happens for a reason.

These animals should be forever-family members; they shouldn't be passed around like a pawn. When you call them your partner, they should really be just like a spouse—someone you commit to for life.

What plans do you have for Zini's non-jumping future?

I've discovered he's great on trails. The first time out he was perfect, so brave and confident. He was happy to have someone on his back and to have a job. Also, I have found a trick trainer in Ocala who I'm going to work with and teach him some tricks.

CHAPTER 13

Read This If Your Friend or Family Member Has Just Lost a Horse

IT'S DEVASTATING TO lose a horse. Even if the horse is not your own, the pain can be multiplied since you are sad for your friend or family member and sad for losing a special horse you knew. Sometimes it's tricky to figure out how to act or what to say. Here are some practical tips gleaned from my own experience losing DC and from talking to a number of horse friends who have also lost a horse.

For starters, whatever you do, please, please, please, refrain from telling your loved one, "I know how you feel ..." and then go on to talk about when you lost a parakeet, dog or even a horse. This is not the time to share your sad story. This is the time to simply be there for your friend.

What Should I Say?

Some better things to say than "I know how you feel"—because you don't—would be, "I'm so sorry," or "This is the worst, but I'm here for you," and even, "If you want to talk about it, I'm available to you. If you don't want to talk about it, I understand."

Artist Emily McDowell has a line of awkward sympathy/empathy cards that allow card-givers the chance to tell it like it is when communicating with their bereaved friend. For example, there's the "I wish I could take away your pain, or at least take away the people who compare it to when their hamster died."

The following statements are **not** comforting for horse lovers grieving their best friend:

"He lived a good life."

"I know exactly how you feel."

"Time heals all wounds."

"When do you think you'll get another horse?"

Heart-felt words, even if they are few, mean a great deal. And a warm embrace can sometimes communicate all the right sentiments without using any words.

What Should I Do?

A few days following DC's death, I received a card in the mail from the barn owner, and it had a few other signatures.

I still have that card, ten years later.

That horse sympathy card didn't ease the pain, but it reminded me there were other people thinking of me and supporting me in my devastation.

If you can't find a horse sympathy card in a tack shop near you, here are some other options for horse sympathy cards:

Etsy has dozens of horse sympathy cards—just search for "horse sympathy card." You'll find some with quotes and some with ethereal horses galloping in the distance. There are really all kinds of styles.

If you're an artsy-craftsy person, you can make your own unique sympathy card.

The online shop of Hunt Seat Paper Co. has a horse sympathy card sharing the message "Horses Always Go to Heaven." (Find it at www.huntseatpaperco.com.)

If you can't find a horse sympathy card near you and you don't want to wait for shipping for an online card, it's okay to use a pretty blank card and write your own message. The design of the card is secondary to the thoughtfulness and empathy demonstrated by sending it.

When Is the Best Time to Deliver a Horse Sympathy Card?

One last point about the horse sympathy card. Timing is key, but you don't have to deliver the card within 24 hours. Even getting a card within a few weeks would be helpful. There's really never a wrong time to express your love and sorrow to a bereaved equestrian friend.

Financial Donation or Gift

One of my friends lost her heart about a year ago. He was in his 30s and in great health, but then he got sick and there was nothing the vet could do. I felt horrible because I knew the pain of losing a heart horse. The sweet bay gentleman gelding was her sunshine—the horse that brought her back to horses after a 10-year hiatus.

Because he was an off-track Thoroughbred, I made a donation to a local OTTB organization in his name. I asked if they could send a letter to my friend stating a donation was made in honor of her horse. I honestly don't know if that's something the organization regularly does, but they were happy to do so.

If you know your friend has a favorite non-profit related to horses or even the wider world of animals, you could make a similar donation. I felt good writing the check and I know my friend was moved by the gesture.

In some cases, losing a horse is extremely expensive. Depending on the circumstances, your friend could have a vet bill for thousands of dollars. If this is the case with your horse lover, and you have the financial means, writing a check to your friend or giving cash is a thoughtful way to show you care.

When I lost DC, my parents wrote the check to pay for my final vet bill. They were in a position to help relieve the financial burden. I've never forgotten their kindness.

Invitation to Ride Your Horse or Just to Lunch

Often the best way to show a hurting person you care is simply by being there. Spending time with your friend is a gift. Depending on the situation, if your friend doesn't have other horses to ride and you do, you could invite them to spend some barn time with you. I would probably wait about a week or two, but even a simple invitation, such as, "I would love to have you come out and take a spin on Dobbin when I go to the barn soon. You can let me know when you're ready," will mean so much.

As referenced earlier, everyone grieves differently, but a simple, heartfelt invitation will demonstrate your kindness and concern in a powerful way. It's a wonderful thing to be invited and feel included. When I lost DC, I felt like the whole world of everything I loved most was shut off to me. I had no desire to return to his barn, but I hadn't lost my passion for all things horse.

And you don't have to start with an invitation to ride. You could just express that you want to connect with your friend along the lines of, "I know it's been a hard time. I'd love to take you out to lunch and we can talk about horses or not. It would be good to see you and spend time together."

Impromptu Stall Memorial

I've walked down the aisle of a barn more than once and noticed an empty stall with an impromptu memorial. The horse's blanket is draped over what I'm guessing was a bucket in the middle of the stall. Flowers are nestled in their grocery store bouquet packing and scattered on top of and around the blanket. I didn't know the horse or owner in these cases, but I was touched by the gesture. What it meant to me was a community of fellow horse lovers reverberated with grief on behalf of a horse and owner pair that were parted. Depending on your friend's horse's barn situation, that could be a fitting tribute as well.

From sending a card to meeting for lunch or extending an invitation to ride, myriad ways exist to show our grieving horse friends our support. Pick one or more ways to show you care. Your kindness will be appreciated and treasured.

Chapter 13 Optional Assignment (for Friend or Relative to Complete)

- Send a card or letter expressing your sympathy, even if you have shared your condolences in person. Jot down a fun memory you have with your friend and their horse.
- If you want a greater challenge, make a donation to a horse-related organization that is meaningful to your friend.

APPENDIX A

My Horse DC's Eulogy

Hello Friends,

This week I am mourning the loss of a great friend/awesome horse of 16 years, DC. He was the light of my life and a source of joy to so many people—my mom, sister Linda, niece, shareboarder, friend Gail, and so many more friends and horse lovers who met him throughout the years in both IL and CA.

On Monday I made the hard decision for DC to be put down as a result of injuries he received from choking.

He was taken to an equine hospital to see if a colic surgery would be an option—the initial diagnosis by the vet who came to the barn was that he colicked. When the hospital vet assessed him, she said he had choked on something (she didn't know what—maybe a wad of hay) and it had gotten into his lungs. That was the real problem, which somehow led to the colic. The vet said she wasn't optimistic he could handle the anesthesia to perform the colic surgery and his various systems were not functioning well due to the stress of the choking. I asked her what she would do if he were her horse—she said it was such a hard decision to make, but she would have put him down.

The Tower Hill Farm barn manager Carrie, the person who called me at 3:45 a.m. Monday, had trailered him to the hospital to see if surgery was an option. Carrie lives at and runs the barn and knows DC. She agreed with me euthanasia was the right decision. She said DC didn't outwardly seem to be in any pain and he was very stoic—not his normal personality. While driving the 5 freeway in the dark, on the way to work, tears streaming down my face, I told Carrie to tell him I loved him, and he had been such a good boy. With tears in her voice she said she would.

When I bought him, I remember feeling guilty that I was depleting my savings account to buy a horse—it seemed so extravagant. A woman at my first job gave me a piece of advice when I shared with her my tentativeness. She said, "Susan, my best friend just died of breast cancer and she was only 40. I think you should buy that horse and enjoy every minute you have with him. Life is short."

And so I did. And I have now just turned 40 myself.

My trainer Joanne "found" DC for me and nudged me to buy him when I wasn't really interested in getting a horse, as I was happily shareboarding one. But I'm so grateful I made the plunge! My mom gave me the $3,750 I needed to pay for half of DC. She always wanted a horse when she was a girl.

Through career changes and relationship ups and downs, DC was a constant. That beautiful brown face with the backward question mark blaze always made me happy. When I would ride him, especially at the canter—his most buoyant and animated gait—I sometimes would get the giggles because he was so exuberant and it was so much fun. I felt like a kid without a care in the world. Being on his back or in the aisle brushing him or standing around holding his lead rope as he grazed was priceless therapy. It's hard to feel lonely, bored, depressed, or sad when you are in the presence of such a powerful, lovely creature that is part wild and yet listens to you and can return affection.

He just had a full exam this July the week before my wedding to see if the vet thought a 23-year old horse should be trailered from IL back to CA. She said, "He's in great health and he doesn't know he's 23. Keep working him. I think he'll be fine."

I'd been trying to find a stable near my new house that would have provided him with an awesome environment for his golden years. Unfortunately, my part of California is so heavily populated that there are virtually no barns with pasture turn out—or at least none I have found at this point.

So I'm happy to know DC's last days were spent grazing in a field with his horse friends in the Midwest. He was Kentucky-born, and he belonged in a grassy pasture.

When I spoke to the hospital vet, I thanked her, and she said I should be happy I gave DC such a good home.

"He was a Thoroughbred, right? Lots of those horses don't end up with a happy story with the same owner for so many years."

Maybe sometime down the road I'll be able to provide another happy ending for another noble Thoroughbred.

I'm grateful to have so many beautiful memories of my beloved horse. I even got a new nose thanks to him!

Attached is a picture taken at a horse show at Lamplight Equestrian Center from the summer of 2005. He really was photogenic and every bit as handsome as his show name, "Adonis," suggests.

Thank you for reading this horse obituary. Thank you for being a special part of my past and present.

Love,
Susan

APPENDIX B

Eulogy Template

Who are the people you'd like to inform about your horse's passing?
(Possible options: previous owner, friends from barns where you used to ride or board, people you know from horse shows, your relatives, farrier, chiropractor, past or current trainers, neighbors)

What details surrounding your horse's death are you comfortable sharing? (Write as little or as much as you'd like for this one.)

Retell the story of how you found your horse. Share how long you had been together.

Add in a picture or several that best exemplify your relationship.

Tell a story or two that you want to always remember about how special your horse was.

Did he or she have a funny habit or quirk? A favorite snack? Best friend?

Close with a meaningful word of appreciation for the people reading your message and caring about both you and your horse.

Notes

1. "The Health Benefits of Tears." *Psychology Today.* Accessed November 06, 2018. www.psychologytoday.com/us/blog/emotional-freedom/201007/the-health-benefits-tears.

2. Govender, Serusha. "Crying: The Health Benefits of Tears." WebMD. Accessed November 10, 2018. www.webmd.com/balance/features/is-crying-good-for-you#2.

3. Pollack, Cameron. "What Do Tears Look Like?" NPR. November 29, 2018. Accessed November 01, 2018. www.npr.org/sections/pictureshow/2018/11/29/668192576/photographer-maps-emotional-terrain-one-tear-at-a-time.

4. Moga, Jeannine, M.A., M.S.W., LICSW. Coping With the Loss of a Horse. Report. Equine Center, University of Minnesota.

Resources

Saddle Seeks Horse Commemoration Resources Page
I've created a dedicated page on my blog with a roundup of ideas to commemorate a dearly departed horse.
saddleseekshorse.com/commemorating-your-horse

The Association of Pet Loss and Bereavement
The Association of Pet Loss and Bereavement has a state directory of pet loss support groups. Many of the groups meet weekly or twice a month. In addition, there are trained pet bereavement counselors available in the chat room.
www.aplb.org

ASPCA Pet Loss Hotline and Grief Website
ASPCA Pet Loss Hotline 1-877-GRIEF-10; www.pet-loss.net

Podcast Interviews
Horse Hour Podcast
"Saying Goodbye to My Best Friend" July 10, 2017 and "Saying Goodnight Forever" December 7, 2015

For Readers in the UK, Blue Cross
www.bluecross.org.uk/pet-bereavement-and-pet-loss

A Helpful Book
The Grief Recovery Handbook by John W. James and Russell Friedman

Acknowledgements

A special heaping of gratitude goes out to Amy, Lauren, Laurie, Melina, and Stephanie for sharing their stories in the hopes of easing the pain of fellow horse lovers, letting them know they are not alone.

And a big thank you and hugs for Allison, Haley, Trenace and other beta readers for helping me refine this message for our equestrian community. You ladies rock!

And speaking of rock, thank you to my rock star designer, editor, artist (that's you, Kasia), and photographers. Your gifts inspire me and will touch the heart of every person who happens upon this book. Thank you from the bottom of my heart.

Author's Note & Contact Info

Thank you for reading *Strands of Hope*. I appreciate you taking the time to journey with some of my horse friends and me as we discussed this heavy topic of losing a horse. I hope you or someone you know (if you got the book to share with a friend) feels less alone as a result of having entered these pages. I just wish I could give hugs in real life and listen to stories of all these much-loved horses.

If you would like to connect, here's where you can find me:

- Email susan@saddleseekshorse.com
- My email newsletter to stay in the loop saddleseekshorse.com/sign-up
- On the blog Saddle Seeks Horse www.saddleseekshorse.com
- Saddle Seeks Horse Facebook Page www.facebook.com/SaddleSeeksHorse
- Instagram www.instagram.com/saddleseekshorse
- Pinterest www.pinterest.com/saddlseekshorse

If you felt *Strands of Hope* was helpful, it would mean so much to me if you would leave a review on Amazon or Goodreads. Reviews are gold for authors like me as they allow more exposure to new readers. And word-of-mouth recommendations are wonderful too. Thanks for being so kind!

LOVING HORSES CAME EASY.

DATING AND FINDING SOMEONE TO LOVE WAS HARD.

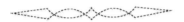

Trot along with Susan in her horse lover's dating memoir and you might fall for someone tall, dark and handsome — and 16.3 hands!

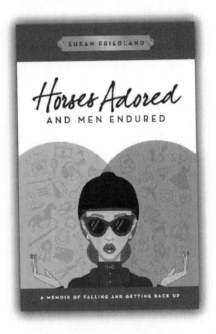

Horses Adored and Men Endured is a charming collection of dating fiascos and horsey tales.

Let's Stay Connected!

You're invited to stay in the horsey loop with me.

Trot along on the blog where I share equestrian information and inspiration for horse lovers like us. Visit the link below to subscribe.

saddleseekshorse.com/sign-up

Tally ho - Susan

Made in the USA
Middletown, DE
07 December 2022